The Happiest You

(Taking You from Jobs, Fatigue, Spouse, Kids, and Stress to Your Talent, Appreciation, and Wealth)

Tammy Mayo, M.D.

ISBN 979-8-88943-467-2 (paperback)
ISBN 979-8-89345-643-1 (hardcover)
ISBN 979-8-88943-468-9 (digital)

Christian Faith Publishing
832 Park Avenue
Meadville, PA 16335
www.christianfaithpublishing.com

Printed in the United States of America

Well, my patients have been telling me I should write a book. My spouse says I should write a book. I have been thinking of writing a book. Well, here it is.

Are you living a life of dread? Wake up, go to work, come home, cook, kids, spouse, stress, drop in bed like a zombie, and sleep—the sleep of the dead for five short hours—then wake up and do it all over again?

What is your purpose here? Did you even know you had a purpose?

Are you broke? Are you living paycheck to paycheck? Is work unfulfilling? Are you tired of your coworkers? Are you tired of your boss? Are you tired of that job? Are you just tired?

How are things at home with your spouse? Are you going to the same places all the time, watching the same shows, eating the same food, doing the same activities, meeting the same friends that you don't really want to talk to anyway?

Have you been on vacation lately? Where would you go if you could? Have you ever been on vacation? Do you know what vacation means?

Are you depressed? Are you filled with anxiety about bills, people, events, and life?

If you answered yes to a lot of these questions, this book is for you. This book will not fix your life. This book will not fix your life. This book will not fix your life. Did you get it? But this book will help fix you in the way that you think about yourself so that *you* can fix your life. This is a book about finding and loving yourself. I wrote this book with very simple terminology, and it is short! So you don't have an excuse not to read it.

Have you met *you*? Do you know who *you* are? Do you know *your* place in this world?

My name is Dr. Tammy Mayo. I have been practicing medicine for twenty years. I absolutely love people. I absolutely love my job. I have fun and laugh all day every day. I'm doing what I was put on earth to do.

I've known that I was going to be a doctor since the age of eight years old. My mother loved to tell the story. Every time one of my friends got hurt, there I was, with alcohol and bandages. I naturally gravitated toward anyone that was injured or upset—always willing to help. I had a happy childhood. I came out of the delivery room laughing. I laughed through infancy, toddler age, and elementary school. I was still laughing in middle school. There were some major challenges when my family moved out of state at the age of thirteen. I went into a different ethnic experience. Here I was, an outsider. The children often remarked that I danced and talked and dressed differently. It took about four to five years, but I eventually found my niche, found friends that appreciated me, and I was right back to laughing again. High school was easy because I enjoyed it. College was easy because I expected it to be easy. Even though I maintained jobs while in college and medical school, I still enjoyed my experiences there. Of course, med school was a lot more difficult than anything I had ever been exposed to. But eventually, I made my way. I did one year of general surgery internship. That internship was distressing because I was around residents that were exhausted from lack of sleep and were over-worked. I switched fields to family medicine and found my happiness and joy yet again. Each major crossroad in my life was an easy decision because I already knew where I was going. Unfortunately, I frequently come across many people that do not feel like I do about their life. They are unhappy. So many unhappy, unhealthy people. My heart goes out to them. I touch as many people as I can. I can only touch fifteen to twenty patients a day. I want to do more. I want to reach more people. So I decided, after being told by so many people to write a book, that I should absolutely do it.

I will tell many case stories in this book. Hopefully these people will be similar enough to you that their story will touch you and change your life. I don't have any magic tricks, no magic medications, and no fancy prayers or chants. What I do have are some situations, questions, and statements that may help you to get to the real you—the happy you. The *you* that you used to be when you were a child, or teenager, or a fiancé. When were you last the happiest of your life? Are you the happiest now? Were you ever happy?

The famous singer Beyoncé says that "she woke up like this." I'm assuming she means beautiful. But I have to tell you, I woke up like this. I mean, in my happy state. Every single day that I wake up, I'm happy, grateful, and loving. No daily alarm clock. When I first wake up, I think of all the things that I'm grateful for, and I thank God. Next, I put on my music, do my yoga stretches, and get moving. I dress myself, drink my coffee, and eat my breakfast—all leisurely and filled with joy and gratefulness.

How do you wake up? Does the alarm frighten you out of a good dream? Is someone rudely shaking you awake? Worse yet, is someone shouting at you to wake you up? Well, let's change that starting today. If you need to be up at six, go to sleep with enough time to give yourself enough sleep so that you can wake up without an alarm. You may need to go to sleep and wake up at the same time every day, including weekends. If you're working shift-work, this could be harder, but you should not have your shifts mixed with days and nights. That will be harder for you to have a good sleep pattern. If you must use an alarm, use an exciting, energetic song that you love instead of a nuclear war siren. Sleep is very important. Remember that the body is healing itself from the day beating during sleep. If you're not getting good rest, it's going to be hard to tackle stress, people, jobs, situations, kids, and life.

Come along and turn the page. Let's go discover and meet the happiest you.

The Best Job in the World

Do you love your job? Is it the best job in the world as far as you are concerned? Would you get up and work for that job for free, six to eight hours a day? If you answered yes to these questions, go to the next chapter. If you answered no to these questions, come with me.

Most jobs require eight to twelve hours a day of your time: Monday through Friday. So this is a third to a half of your day, five days a week. If your job is not good for you, you need to leave. If you don't wake up happy to go to work, happy to interact with your coworkers, happy to interact with the customers, then you need to leave.

Does your boss appreciate you? Does your boss appreciate your input? Or is your boss rude, demanding, and unappreciative? Changing jobs is a big decision. But because we spend so much of our life at work, it's a decision that can change your life. I have seen people with miserable jobs. I'm seeing people very depressed over the job that they're holding. I've seen people having panic attacks at the idea of having to go back to work on Monday. Step 1, of course, is not to take a job that you know will make you miserable. If you can't stand the smell of paint, don't go work in a paint factory. Do not allow personal circumstances and financial situations to put you in a place that's going to destroy your mental sanity.

Step 2 is as soon as you realize that you're going to have major problems with a coworker, go discuss it with the boss. Some people may choose to discuss it with a coworker, that's your decision. The point is to discuss it with someone because if you don't, this problem could get drastically worse. Do not allow this situation to go on for long periods of time. If the boss can't do anything, ask for one of you to be moved, either them or you. Make a lateral move: move up, move down, just move!

Step 3 is to make sure that you are wanted and appreciated by your boss. If you aren't, this could create problems with your duties, promotions, raises, and moving up in the company. If you see that there is going to be a major problem with your boss, ask for a move: lateral, up, and down. Just move! Do not allow this to go on for a long time. A vindictive, evil boss can make your life a living hell. Don't even let this begin to happen. A patient once told me that his two bosses were making his life miserable with demands and such. I told him it's probably not personal. He countered that they had directly told him that it was personal. Now, folks, this does not take an MD to figure out. Why continue working for two people that have already told you that they dislike you? His excuses were financial. I think it had more to do with self-hatred. When you have to go to the doctor to get medication in order to stay on a job, that is definitely not the job for you. This is not rocket science.

Perhaps the problem is too large of a workload. You'll need to discuss this with your boss or coworkers. Delegate if you can. Ask for an extension on the time. Whatever you do, you need to do something. Otherwise, a prolonged heavy workload can cause severe stress and anxiety, lack of sleep, and increased blood pressure. It's not worth it. Perhaps you are the star supervisor! Everybody counts on you. Everybody delegates to you because they know you are the best, and you will get the job done! You're working late hours, you're working on weekends, you're working on holidays, and you're working on your kids' birthdays! If this job is requiring drugs to keep you going, you need to delegate some of this responsibility. I don't want to see you in urgent care with a heart attack. Do not allow this stress and responsibility to put you in the hospital. I tell my patients, "IF YOU DROP DEAD, THAT COMPANY WILL REPLACE YOU and probably by next week." It's not worth it. You are taking years off of the back end. That's right, the back end of your life. It's not worth it!

I hear you whining, "But Dr. Mayo, I can't afford to quit this job. I am living paycheck to paycheck. My kids need food and a roof over their heads. This job is paying for everything." To this, I rebuttal, "You can't afford *not* to quit this job! If you drop-dead, no one is going to be paying for the food and the rent anyway. Get yourself together. Maybe you have to put a little bit aside for a few months until you can afford a down payment somewhere else. You can move in with a friend or relative for one or two months until you get the next job. Better yet, look for another job while you're at this job! Make a smooth transition. But you must do something. You might suffer for a few months, but even happily suffering with a plan is better than sustaining torture somewhere breaking down your mental stability. Put in your head the job that you want and go get it!"

If you're working overnight and you have young kids and you aren't spending any time with them, you need a different job. If you can't afford things that you want and need, you need a different job. If you just got demoted unjustly, you need a different job. If your back is hurting every night when you get home from work, you need a different job (or a better back).

I often hear people say that they don't know what job they really want. I recommend searching your hobbies. If you enjoy painting, become a painter. If you enjoy thrilling heart-wrenching adventures, be an adventure tour guide. Be a professional bungee jumping coach. I met a young girl who had been expelled from school and was in a detention center for fighting. She told me that she likes to fight. I recommended that she start training to become a boxing coach right away or a boxer. There's something for everyone. There is a job for you no matter what crazy activity you like to do. And guess what, you can even become a millionaire doing it. You understand what I mean? If you enjoy baking, teach baking classes, or start a baking cook show. Look at your top three hobbies. I always say your job should be something that you would not mind doing for free. You've probably heard that a lot, but it is so true. You can make a business out of almost any job or talent. I strongly believe that you can get rich doing any job. You might have to own a business doing the job, but nevertheless, you can make a lot of money doing almost anything. Look at how much money people made by just picking up our trash each day. Now go out and use your creativity.

I'm sure I don't have to tell you that there are hundreds of self-made millionaires that did not graduate from college, or even go to college. So don't allow that as an excuse either. Making money and getting the job that you want has more to do with your determination and drive as opposed to your education. Do something that you love. Choose something that will help other people in this world in some way. Perhaps you're helping people gain an hour more of time for themselves each day: helping with food, helping with fresh ideas, technology, assistance—you name it. It's easier to manifest a job when your goal is to help others. One of my young patients told me that she could not get the job she wanted because she could not afford to go to college. Haberdash! Nonsense! Go look at YouTube videos and figure it out. As long as you know how to do it well, you can create the job that you want doing what you love. Remember, I told you this. If this makes you a millionaire in the future, please send me a little something.

CHAPTER 2

Why Are You So Tired?

You're waking up tired. You're going to sleep tired. You're yawning at your child's recital. You are easy to anger and irritable. You are yelling at the kids and your spouse. You don't have enough energy to get up those three flights of stairs. Why are you so tired? You're taking the vitamins. You're trying to exercise. You're drinking energy drinks and coffee galore, and you're still tired. Sometimes I have patients that come and complain of fatigue. I always ask them three things: What are you eating?

How much are you sleeping? Are you depressed or stressed out? Now of course there are other medical problems that can cause fatigue. But these three are the basics. When you're eating a high carbohydrate diet, the food is only giving you short bursts of energy, then you crash. Please make sure you're eating three servings of vegetables a day at least! Do not ask me what vegetables are! Also, protein needs to be in the diet as well.

Now of course you're going to need sleep. The two main absolute things the body requires for proper functioning are food and rest. You may not need eight hours of sleep. I usually recommend five to eight hours for adults. Everyone doesn't need this much sleep, but if you're tired all day, then you do. The flipside of sleep is exercise. The body does need activity during the day. This could be simple walking. I'm not telling you to run five miles a day. That's not necessary. Movement is necessary though. If you sit and watch TV for three hours a day, you might not sleep well, and then you'll be tired the next day.

So you've eaten and you've slept. But lo and behold, your mind is troubled. Depression and stress can cause oversleeping and insomnia. Yes, it can cause both. Some simple questions you can ask yourself to determine if you're clinically depressed are:

- Sleeping too much, or inability to sleep?
- Overeating, or loss of appetite?
- Feeling depressed, down, and hopeless?
- Feeling worthless, or that you let people down?
- Loss of desire for pleasurable activities?
- Suicidal ideation?
- Isolating yourself?

If you have these criteria, you should see your doctor or psychologist or psychiatrist.

Now, on the other hand, if you wake up with the chickens, with a smile on your face and joy in your heart, join me in singing along to my morning jam's playlist. Come on, let's go cook some grits, eggs, and bacon—my favorite weekend breakfast!

CHAPTER 3

Stress

The famous Yogi Sadhguru said that when he came to America, he could not believe people were trying to manage stress. He said he didn't understand why someone would want to manage stress instead of just getting rid of it. I totally agree. Life is not perfect. We all have ups and downs, bumps in the road, stressors, and changes. All these things that happen are simply life. Sadhguru teaches that you cannot expect life to be perfect, and if you do, then you should immediately find your way to heaven because you are not equipped to live on earth. Although his teachings sound a little harsh here, he has a good point. You cannot expect life to be without change or difficulties. It's part of what makes life, life. We cannot change this. We cannot change things from happening. But what we can change is our response to the situation. We can decide that we are not going to let something ruin our day, our week, or our life. When a difficult situation arises, you must make a decision on how to deal with it. Pull any lessons from it that you can. Try to see any goodness that may come out of it in the end. And then move on. Yes, that's right. You must move on. You do not have my permission to sulk, nor extend the torture.

Step 1 is to determine your major stressors. If this is a job, you need to make a lateral move. Move up, move down, move out, quit, resign, or retire. You could also reduce your hours, you can change the days you're working to weekends instead, you could move to nights instead, you could move to another state, etc.

Let's say your stressor is a certain family member. You need to immediately begin to limit your exposure to this family member or friend. Limit conversations on the phone. Pick your own personal time limit. It might be ten minutes, or it might be twenty minutes. Limit interactions socially where this person will be involved. You could go to the party but leave after an hour and try to limit your time speaking to that person. You could drop the friend altogether. Sometimes, we have to decrease exposure to family members if they are very angry, inflammatory, or stress-inciting. If they're particularly bad or argumentative, you could limit your interactions to text messaging only. Thank goodness for technology.

If your stress is a spouse or child, see the next two chapters.

Lastly, learn how to put things into perspective. Sometimes, when things happen that we title as negative, it might really be something positive. Many times, there are positive lessons or outcomes that come out of a bad situation. You got laid off from the job. You thought it was going to kill you because your rent was two months late after that. Now eight months later, you have not only a better job, but better hours, higher pay, and it's closer to your house. And you have the weekends off. Sit back and be grateful. Just take the time to evaluate something the next time it seems very bad. Situations are not truly bad; it is just how we look at them. I know someone who lost a high-paying job and had to move to a different city. Now their children are doing much better in school, and they have an even better job and more time with their children. Sometimes, you just have to sit back and evaluate. Try to see the good in the change, whatever it may be.

CHAPTER 4

Kids, You Gotta Love 'Em

I am deeply in love with my two children. I think they're the best two kids in the entire world. If you don't feel the same about your children, please read on.

Your children should be a source of major joy for you. If they're infants, they smell so good and they're so cuddly you just want to see them smile and laugh and hug them all day. If they're toddlers, you have to watch them 24-7, but you love to watch their milestones slip by. If they're in middle school, make sure they're not being bullied and help them with their homework. If they're in high school, watch out. This is a time the children are beginning to move toward her adulthood, and they should be learning about responsibility. They're trying to make decisions. They're trying to become the person that they were put here on earth to be. Let them do it. Don't interfere. Simply guide them. Make sure they have the basics: proper sleep, eating healthy, studying in school, if necessary. Guide them. Do not try to control them. If you do, trouble is right around the corner. Also, their hormones are raging. They really need your support right now, not dictatorship. Don't criticize their friends, their hair, their clothing, or their music. These are all expressions of their individuality. Let them become them. They're not supposed to become you exactly. Of course, if they're doing something illegal, yes, you should step in. Otherwise, assist, support, guide, and most important of all, love them. That's what they need from us: love and acceptance.

Next our high schoolers are out and in college. Keep in mind they are young adults. They are no longer forced to honor your ideals or rules. Respect them as their own person. If they're living with you, give them some responsibility and lay down your rules as necessary. They will need responsibility if they're living with you because they couldn't go anywhere else and live for free without paying any utilities or rent. Whatever you do, do not allow them to be rude to you or disrespectful. They wouldn't be able to do that out in the real world to a landlord, right? Don't butt heads. If they don't want to follow your rules or respect you, give them a time frame that they can move to their own apartment or house and rule their own roost. Of course, if you need to help them a little bit, do so. But what you will not do is allow them to cause you undue stress, high blood pressure, high blood sugars, heart attacks, stroke, and death.

All in all, remember, the kids are a wonderful joy. It's so fun to watch them grow up and grow into the adult that they are meant to be.

CHAPTER 5

Spouse: Love-Hate Relationships

Well, you and your spouse are having lots of problems? It can happen. Communication is necessary. I highly recommend marriage counseling. One person being driven and going to see the psychiatrist is not going to fix the marriage. Both of you must go. It doesn't have to be a psychiatrist. No one necessarily needs to take medications. Communication is key. Also, two stones cannot come together. People must bend and be flexible in order to maintain a relationship. If violence or drugs is part of the relationship, I do recommend separation and counseling. If you have gotten to the point where you're having high blood pressure, blood sugars, stress, anger, and insomnia, you have to do something different.

Your spouse should be your best friend. The person that you can talk to about anything. The person that you can hug and cuddle up with when it's cold and raining outside. The person that you enjoy life with. Someone who is there for you when you are sick. Someone you can laugh with. Someone you can cry with. Your better half. If you're not feeling respected and supported, you really need to discuss this. After counseling and giving it a serious try, you may need to separate and go your own ways. Whatever you decide, you do need to be happy at home, with or without this person. You can rebuild, or you can meet someone else. Your life will not end without this person. Step back and take a good look at the situation. You must accept responsibility for your half of the relationship. Look at what you're doing. Try to see things from their standpoint. If you can't see things from their view, then enlist the counselor to help out. Good luck.

Your Talent

Why are you here? Why were you put on earth? Do you know your cause? We all are put on earth for a reason. This, I truly believe. Everyone has their personal talent. Everyone should know their reason for existence. Some of us learn this as children or teenagers; others of us learn as adults. Either way, you need to start looking for your reason, and you need to find it ASAP. In order to live the most fulfilling life, you have to know your reason for being here. It doesn't have to involve money. Whatever activity it is, it's going to be something that you absolutely love to do. It is going to improve society and other people's lives. You are going to feel wonderful and fulfilled performing this said activity. My reason for living was to become a doctor. I am so grateful that I was given my pathway as a child. I believe it made my life easier. You must discover yours. Think of your hobbies. Think of the things you really love to do. You can excel in this activity. Your life will be so fulfilling and wonderful. You will love to do this activity every day. You will want to do it as much as possible. Go find your talent and find true happiness.

CHAPTER 7

Are You Grateful?

Dr. Norman Peale in *The Power of Positive Thinking* came across a man who had lost a lot of money and was complaining that he didn't have anything. Dr. Peale quickly reminded him of simple things that he was taking for granted: his wife, his children, his friends, and his health. I see people every day that are complaining about certain things. Most of the time, I'm thinking to myself, *This person has sight, beauty, intelligence, children, a spouse, a car, a house, a job. How lucky they are! Not to mention, the ability to hear, smell, taste, touch, to enjoy all that our Mother Earth has to offer.*

I usually recommend that as soon as you wake up, before you even open your eyes, start counting off a few things that you are grateful for. Think back and remember the funny joke your spouse told you the day before. What about the fact that you missed that car accident by a hair on the way to work last week? Your child brought his failing math grade up to a *B* or *C.* Your back injury didn't bother you this week. Your mother's still alive. Your father's still alive. Your daughter didn't marry that guy. You know, the one you didn't like. You saw the sunset yesterday evening. It was beautiful. It finally rained, and your plants got the water that they needed. The work schedule had you off work Saturday and Sunday! *Woo-hoo*! Your girlfriend invited you to dinner to meet her parents. I could go on and on and on. Just simply lying there and feeling grateful for a few minutes can really get your day started off on a good foot. The next time you are thinking about complaining about something, instead, think about all the things that you have to be grateful for.

Once you start counting, you will find that there are many more things to be grateful for than there are to complain about.

CHAPTER 8

Manifesting and Meditating

I'm only going to talk about these two things for a minute. I will talk more about it in my next book. I've had a wonderful life: a fulfilling life filled with joy and love. I give a lot of love, and I believe that is why I receive so much love. I thank God for my happiness.

I would like to end this book with the idea that *you* are responsible for everything that happens in your life. I get to love and have had a good life because, in my mind, this is what I deserve and what I am due. I believe we all deserve a good happy life with inner peace. One thing people have trouble with is accepting the responsibility that what happens in life is, in some part, due to their own thinking or thought process. In the Bible, when the two groups of men were sent to survey the promised land, one group came back with the information that it was a land flowing with milk and honey. The second group reported that there were giants inhabiting the land and that they were unable to proceed. I'm saying that situations in life can be evaluated differently, depending on the person. Try to see the good in life at all times.

Friends and coworkers have remarked to me in the past that I'm so lucky. They have reported that I am a rich doctor, and that is why I have such a good life. Unbeknown to them, I know plenty of rich doctors that are absolutely miserable. Also I've been bankrupt twice. Luck is not how I got here, but neither is severely hard work, IT'S MY MENTALITY! *I believe* that I should always live a good life, and therefore, I do. I believe that God, or the universe, will take care of me and my children, and so we are provided for.

I recommend meditating for fifteen minutes per day. Some people call this silent praying. Simply sit down, close your eyes, relax, and let go. Try to think of nothing. Try to accept and be open to ask for instruction from God or the universe or your subconscious mind when you're dealing with a serious decision. Your mama, sister, cousin, or best friend do not always have the best advice for you. Trust your own instinct. You know yourself and your situation better than anyone on this planet. Relax and take time to clear your mind so that the right decision will come to you.

Envision and imagine yourself having the best life that you want, the best job, the best spouse, and it, or they, will come. If you want something to change in your life, envision what it is that you want. See yourself in your new house, driving your new car, or having good friends that you can trust. You create your own life through your thoughts.

Hopefully you can use the ideas that I've set forth in this book and find the happiest you!

In my next book, I will go into further detail about how I *stay* happy.

Put your happiness above all else! Only by following this creed can you be the best for the ones you love. Until my next book, stay *The Happiest You!*

ABOUT THE AUTHOR

Tammy Mayo, MD, has been a medical professional for over twenty years. She has owned three medical practices. She is licensed in two states. Dr. Mayo says, "I have seen almost one hundred thousand patients and enjoyed every minute of it. I have seen a lot of people hurting in today's time. I want to change that, and so I started writing books. I appeal to patients through their daily problems. I want to touch their soul and bring them the joy they deserve."